From Hull
To Adversity

A Collaboration
In Verse.

Val Redmore-McDonald
Sue Ireland
Terry Ireland

The serving soldier.

They do their service, and they leave, but like discarded clothing that retains a body shape, their minds hold the memories that sometimes come back to kick in later life.

These are the authors:

a long service Warrant Officer who experienced sexual discrimination but was told it was 'character building';

the young widow of a Veteran remarried in later life to another Veteran;

the short service Cold War Veteran, junior NCO, who bucked the system and escaped.

Their journeys started in Hull

This is their poetry.

Valerie Redmore-McDonald

A Necklace Of Children's' Fingers
A Poppy Just For Them
Bumpy Jumper
Five Minutes To …..
Paper Football
Passion Killers
Palestinian Genocide
The Lone Irish Ranger
The Allotment Men
The NAAFI Disco
About Turn
Paragon Of Virtue
Ray Of Steel
Our Ted
I'm Over The Rainbow
My Ticket To The World
DIY Why
My Mam's Head
I Bet You Are A Vet
PTSMe

A Necklace Of Childrens' Fingers

I once was told that Civil War
Is really the most cruel
No Boss, no sense, no recompense
Barbarity; no rules

I served in Banja Luka
There are things I can't unsee
Amongst the daily, khaki grind
There was such misery

We laughed and played like soldiers
Drank hard to keep at bay
The horrors that we witnessed
As we went about our day

I had rules of engagement
I had my fellow peers
My training, my Esprit de Corps
Experience of years

But Bosnia was different
Dark clouds descended there
The monsters of society
Allowed to roam and fair

Rich pickings for an evil soul
A playground for the devil
Ive seen some stuff, it's been enough
This was a different level

I met a man, a Warrior
A Warlord - what a King!
His chest displayed his necklace
What a trophy, what a win!

Made up of children's fingers
As he'd tortured, maimed and killed

So proud of his achievements
And the evil he could wield

Sometimes I sit and ponder
Sometimes I sit and cry
I can't unsee the things I've seen
I can't undo my eyes

I once was told that Civil War
Is really the most cruel
No Boss, no sense, no recompense
Barbarity, no rules

A Poppy Just For Them

A Poppy for Remembrance
A Poppy just for them
The blood and bones of faceless men
Entwined upon a stem

We pin them to our outdoor coats
We mount them on our suits
We cannot see their soulless face
Or march inside their boots

Their sacrifice is palpable
The sacrifice unkind
For War has taken many hearts
And ruined many minds

When you pick out your Poppy
Think of who it represents
A Soldier, Sailor, Airman
And the journey underwent

To far flung lands with foreign tongues
No love, no peace for them
Then take the pin, secure it sound
Your Poppy and its stem.

Bumpy Jumper

I've been called Bumpy Jumper
I've had my bottom pinched
My boobs have launched a thousand stares
I've avoided and un-clinched

They've told me I'm not Welcome
We've not had one before
Where will you wash
Where will you eat
A Lesbian or a whore?

Are you grumpy due to monthlies
Will you cry if we shout loud
Make sure you lock your door at night
And don't you make a sound

You females just ain't wanted
You women make me sick
You really can't be soldiers
Cos you haven't got a dick

As time went on I managed
To keep calm and retort
As guys like those, with mini brains
Don't deserve a second thought

If I had been your Daughter
If I had been your wife
Your Mother or your Auntie
Would you still have give me strife

Would you still enjoyed abusing me
Made me small on a parade
With your mindless jokes and your jibes and pokes
Followed by a dark tirade

Yes, Sir - I'm on my monthly
and you're a viscous man
You've made me feel like hell on earth
now release me if you can

I'll just pop to the Armoury
sign out the Duty gun
Then I'll disappear in a splash of blood
You can tell them that you won

Five Minutes To…

A soldier's always early
We're really rather keen
No missing out on action
Ensuring we are seen

Our watch was always perfect
We checked with News at Ten
And if we were still unconvinced
We'd check it all again

For tardiness is chargeable
It screams a million sins
Like - you are unimportant
I am doing better things

No watch now though
To get me there
My mobile phone does fine
With ten alarms and warning bells
'Siri' keeps me on time!

Paper Football

My eyes have seen such horror
My ears have picked up pain
My feet have walked in misery
No-one accepting blame

At night I often wake up sad
And think I'm in a dream
But then I rouse and know it's real
This misery I've seen

Displaced and anxious people
No food or clothes or meds
Children, hollow crying
in dank and filthy beds

No night light; zero power
And dangerous Broken floors
Makeshift curtains, shattered glass
These are the facts of wars

And in the total chaos
The horror that I've seen
A smile can come from nowhere
Grabbed from a sullied scene

A boy had made a football
with paper and with string
And in this crushed and ruined Town
I see his eyes, they sing

He has a disconnection
He's soaring with his soul
His body is ecstatic
As he kicks a World class goal

Passion Killers

In female basic training
You're issued lots of kit
There's shoes and skirts
With khaki shirts
It's all a perfect fit!

But when it comes to leisure wear
It really is a thriller
The Quartermaster excels himself
With issued passion killers

These garments are made of Teflon steel
The elastic is barbed wire
They scratch and itch and do not fit
They're really rather dire

You wear them under a PE skirt
They cut your blood supply
I've seen grown women after sport
Look at their groins and cry

The worst is on an Army run
Especially round the Town
With thirty girls in mini-skirts
Just bobbing up and down

The passion killers cause a stir
For every passing Squaddie
And as you pass you fix your hair
and gently stroke your body

It's strange to say, but if I dare
Suggest it was a coup
To ask a Lady soldier out
and whilst she's in the loo

Go rifling in her knicker drawer
to harness such a steal
Take back this prize
To show the guys
That where you've been was real

On de-kit you are often asked
if you want them and you muster
A "Yes please, Sir! I've just the job
I'll use them as a duster".

Palestinian Genocide

The despair my heart is feeling
The despair my eyes can see
Is the furthest I have ever felt
From today's humanity

My revulsion is unyielding
as the Channels churn out news
With no care for all the suffering that
Attacks my human views

Oh, suffer little children
Let's pour phosphorus on your head
Let's take an innocent woman
and then rape her in her bed

These men cannot be soldiers
These men cannot be sane
This is a horror story
Repeated over and over again

Where are the Guardians of our World?
Where is the moral code?
The international community?
The Statesmen and the bold?

There is just one cruel word for this
Its purely Genocide
The people of the Gaza strip
Have no Homes, and can't hide

As I sit here and type this verse
The people fade away
With bombs and bullets
Knives and gas
There's nothing I can say

If God exists then now's the time
To dig deep and to find
A solution to this man-made-hell
This destruction of mankind

The Lone Irish Ranger

With twinkling eyes and Irish charm
I first saw Roy and felt alarm
For I knew then, as sure can be
That he was mine; just him and me

Port Stanley was a rugged place
With crazy clouds and rain and space
For weeks we loved and laughed and cried
Was never from each other's side

He talked of life in Killyleagh
And how, when older, would one day
Be rich and drive the fastest car
But most of all he loved his Ma

Devoted to his family life
He wanted children and a wife
To settle down in Killyleagh
Until his dying day, he'd say

For Irishmen, it seems to me
Will always cross the Irish Sea
To be with kin, to feel the craic
The wind being always on their back

But sadly, this was not to be
For Roy was fit and tragically
The Regiment coaxed him to Box
My pretty boy took many knocks

One night he paid the final price
His match was off, it wasn't nice
Amid the punches and the roar
Roy fell and never left the floor

He died that night
It was so cruel
A young man's life
Snuffed out,
My jewel
It's many years and still I pray
He made it Home to Killyleagh

The Allotment Men

The Allotment men are normally old, in brown clothes and green wellies. They have wide brimmed hats and Stevie Wonder type sunglasses. The Allotment men are not fashionable.

The Allotment men ride rusty bikes or can drive posh 4WD. The Allotment men travel in their own solitary way. Some push their own wheelbarrows to the plot. Others walk with a cloth bag in hand to put their pickings in.

Allotment men are the protectors of peas, experts in onions the western front of watercress.

The Allotment men rarely smile, hardly never laugh and have a strong, purposeful walk that resonates down the shared pathway, as they traverse to their plot, in a purposeful manner.

The Allotment men are proud, resourceful, innovative and canny. They have bits of string and wire hidden in pockets and pouches like a magician with a coin. The Allotment men mend and stitch their fruit nets and weave care into their cabbage cages with deftness and experience.

The Allotment men have great knowledge. They are totally aware of the waste products from their homes and kitchens. They recycle eggshells and coffee grounds for slug control. They rush daily bodily habits so they can grow carrots in loo roll tubes and kitchen paper holders.

They love breaking down egg cartons for their compost heaps and sometimes they like to germinate baby leeks and onions in them. The Allotment men never waste anything.

The Allotment men aren't keen on women. They pretend they are but they don't like women in their manor.

They see women bending over as they dig up weeds and harvest beans and says things like 'what a view' and Allotment women reply with 'looking at my blackcurrant bush again, Alan?" and then the Allotment men guffaw over rusty fences and pallet style gateways and sidle off.

The Allotment men never hang about after a good guffaw.

The Allotment men have a tool for everything. The spade, the shovel, the fork, the hoe, the Dutch hoe, the onion hoe, the rake, the trowel, the clippers, the pruners. Every tool has a job and the Allotment men will not proceed without the correct tool.

The compost heap in the epicentre of the Allotment men's world.

Here they will discard all that is distasteful to them. Rotting vegetation, broken love affairs, feral children, their own urine (they often pee on it), unpleasant neighbours … the compost heap is the Allotment Men's confessional …here they toss their waste, bad thoughts and regrets of life and as it rots and makes good its sins, they gain a sense of fulfilment and gratitude at their efforts to save all this unwanted matter from the modern emotional and recycling phenomena.

The Allotment men hate waste.

Allotment men are drawn to Allotments as they have left military positions, offices, and factories. They no longer run squadrons, teams, and clients. They have no control left in their life except Brigades of Brassicas and Platoons of peppers. The Allotment men are lost.

This breed of man is a disappearing culture. They don't truly understand reality TV, wokeism, Prince Harry, their grandchildren, their wives or the Kardashians.

The Allotment men will die off soon like Autumn leaves on an apple tree. The Allotment men with blow away in the wind and end up in their own compost heap.

The NAAFI Disco

I love the NAAFI disco
The highlight of my week
Go with the girls
Do disco twirls
And end up cheek to cheek

I'll drink a fancy larger
and partake in sipping schnapps
I don't want to drink many though
And end up on my back

The Guardsmen come in formation
The REME two by two
The ACC do disc-jokey
As I peel off to the loo

The Ladies are still preening
Look gorgeous whilst we can
Then strut out there, without a care
And get us one hot man

The lights are getting softer
The music's getting slow
We pick a prize
Make baby eyes
And wait for him to know

He's seen my weird signals
Considered carnal stare
He casts his eyes, first left then right
Before he's fixed my glare

And slowly he moves forward
Traverses to my space
With military precision
He makes his move with pace

My pal, she sees him coming
She intervenes; she tabs
Oh, Hen, I went with him last week
And now I've got the crabs

My mini-exhilaration
My weekend scene of joy
Has disappeared in clouds of fear
I do not want this boy

But maybe I will see him soon
I'll be happy as can be
He will turn up and I'll scrub up
I work in STD!

About turn!

My Mother told me of the gays
When joining up, and all their ways
She said they were the nicest folk
But leave alone, don't nosey poke

I took her words and made them law
I looked for gays, but did no more
The boys liked me, and I liked them
I knew that I attracted men

As years went on I saw the truth
The hurt the sadness, loss of youth
Crushed careers, shattered, torn
Children yearned for, never born
Not living as they were meant to be
Because they're in the military

And now my Friends are older, proud
Can be themselves; shout PROUD out loud
I'm still sad for Humanity
But they're now
Who they were born to be

Paragon of Virtue

My Dad left Hull in '52
To fight the Commies in Malay
He never spoke to anyone
Except this ornament of clay

He bought it from an antique shop
In London, and it had a name
He called him Bijou, his Gurkha friend
And Bijou listened to his pain

For many years I used to laugh
And listened quietly in my bed
To Dad downstairs, the worse for wear
Emptying the thoughts inside his head

Poor Bijou listening to the tales
of Commie knives and blazing trails
The bugs the bites, the lack of food
The burning Sun, a sombre mood

One day a telegram appeared
His Mam was dying
As he feared
He knew she hadn't been that well
This news released him from fresh hell

He had to clear a landing zone
His jungle knife and him alone
The chopper came and saved his soul
He left his heart in that black hole

Then back to Hull from Singapore
The train arrived, an open door
He knelt and cried, no hesitation
and kissed the floor of Paragon Station

These boys were plucked
from Yorkshire streets
And sent to War with boyhood feet
Jungle warfare, Reds and then
Returned to Hull as hardened men

Dad stayed in Town for 30 years
Until he'd shedded all his fears
Of not being safe and been away
He went to Spain on holiday

Old Bijou sits near my TV
He's older now and funnily
He listens to my tales of War
And smiles quite gently as I snore

Ray of Steel

After years in the Army
I began to want to leave
Every day a struggle
No hunger to achieve

More senior in ranking
Than many of the men
Maybe jealousy or fear
But I felt it now and then

Excluded from the Lads' Nights Out
To Strip Clubs; Russian bars
My visitors were monitored
Took number plates on cars

The foul Commanding Officer
Labelled me "fresh meat"
As I started a dream posting
I then started to retreat

Then one fine day
Arrived my Ray
My Ray, my Ray of steel
He friended me and luckily
Assessed this wasn't real

He said 'it's inappropriate'
For men to be so cruel
They wouldn't like their Daughter
To be spoken to like fools

He gave me the encouragement
to look them in the eye
To say 'you're inappropriate'
Whilst trying not to cry

But honestly, they'd worn me down
Their strength was overpowering
I left the post, went Home a ghost
The whole two years harrowing

My Ray of steel was there for me
He stood right by my side
I faced my foes in a military court
The shame they could not hide

And many females after me
Have shared a similar fate
Been ousted from a job they loved
With such unfounded hate

I hope they found a Ray of Steel
A rock, a friend, a life
We had a pretty messy start
But I'm proud to be his Wife

Our Ted

Our Ted is strong and fierce and loyal
He's fed before our kettle's boiled
His big green eyes, his perfect stare
He melts our heart and we don't care

Our Ted has seen off local cats
And mice and spiders, even rats
Poor Winky cat who lives next door
Has felt the wrath of our Ted's paw

He will present with battle scars
With cuts and chafes and oil from cars
He squeals with joy at our open door
And Husband Ray, with food, gives more

His latest enemy is extreme
He's ginger too and big and mean
He swaggers down the double yellows
He makes a din
Oh, how he bellows

But our Ted will hold his patch
He waits with poise, won't even scratch
Our Ted will sit like he has won
Our Ted is clearly our Son

I'm Over The Rainbow

When the world is a hopeless jumble
When Judy can't make you smile
The scarecrow is Putin
The tin man is shooting
The lion has run off a mile
Just remember that deep in your wardrobe
Amongst all of the clutter and hues
Is a pair of Red,
most divine,
purest shine
forever thine
Sparkling,
thrice Tappable shoes

My Ticket To The World

My Mother always told me
When I sat upon her knee
That the way out of our hum-drum life
Was through the military

We didn't have much money
We didn't have the means
Opportunity was lacking
To escape to different scenes

When I heard of Spandau Ballet
My heart leapt with pure delight
The New Romantic music scene
Just sparkled in the night

The songs fell out the radio
Just landed in my head
And my teenage mindset soaked them up
Whilst laying on my bed

Out of all the New Romantics
Tony Hadley was my King
So True, so cool, so handsome
And boy, could that fella sing

As I commenced my Army life
Spandau with me; bold
Through the Barricades I went
Every day was Gold

Round and Round
Ill fly for you
Highly Strung, Once more
Tony, Martin, Gary
Gently helping me to soar

When they split up
It broke my heart
My Brothers, almost mine
A teenage girl can fall in love
They were my true Lifeline

But I stayed loyal to Tony
I have stalked him to the full
Falklands, Grimsby, Sydney
Dubai, Bosnia and Hull

Some people say I'm crazy
How this passion has unfurled
But I smile and tell them Tony gave me
My Ticket to the World

D I Why?

Men! Who needs them?
No, I say
For I can equal any day
Move a wardrobe, change a plug
Mow the garden, kill a slug
Drink a beer, be a tart
Lie and cheat and break a heart
But when I'm cold and feeling blue
Men! Who needs them?
Guess I do…

My Mam's Head

My Mam's Dementia adventure
Threw problems in the mix
I had to be creative
And pull out my bag of tricks

The most important feature
Though it's not often said
Was the running and the management
Of my poor Mother's head

Her eyes they needed glasses
And testing every year
As Opticians puffed air on her lens
You could almost smell her fear

Her ears needed syringing
And cleaning every week
She'd squirm and wriggle like a bird
With tears down her cheek

Her teeth! Now there's a story
She still owned a full set
An Irish Dentist knocked her out
When she spat and got her wet

Her nostrils needed squirting
When they blocked up in the cold
My God it is a misery
To finally get old

Mam's hair, it needed cutting
A good shampoo and set
But she pulled out all the curlers
And ate the pink hairnet

I often used to mutter
I even had a moan

That if she was Wurzel Gummidge
I'd take her head out on its own

Despite trials and tribulations
And challenges anew
Her fear was real and still her mouth
Would tell me 'I love you'.

I Bet You Are A Vet?

You wake up bright and early
Look forward to the day
The morning routine done and done
The dishes squared away

You have a big to-do list
Kind to people you haven't met
You're booted, suited always muted
I bet you are a Vet?

You own the streets around you
But others live there too
They are an inconvenience
It'd be better with just you

They come and go
You know them
Could set your watch and clock
The fella in the next door flat runs totally amock

But you have sussed his details
You know his plans and creed
You'll put him on the back burner
Retrieve it when you need

The shop upon the corner
You know their rank and name
You like to know the neighbours
Pity they don't do the same

or Civvi Street is coloured beige
The Army life was red
It was filled with fun, by the joyful tonne
It echoes in your head

Thank goodness we have a secret code
We meet and know our mob
We drink and laugh, reminisce and barf
Sometimes we even sob

Ive never met a soldier that I didn't like, as yet
They're smart and sound
I pick them out
I bet you are a Vet?

Sue Ireland

All The Way Home
Jack Harrison VC, MC
Inverary
Wilfred
Jimmy's Place
A Photograph Of Jack Harrison
Parish Register
Endrick Water
Sharon
Hot August Night

All The Way Home

Sometimes it seems too hard to bear
In these trenches, afraid and alone,
I remember my friends and my village
And the loving contentment of home.

I think of my friends and my family
And happier days gone by
I think of the sunset over the fields
The memory makes me cry

And I'm thinking of Dick, Tom and Harry
Jimmy and George and Will Chance
My friends, my childhood companions
Now forever asleep here in France

And I look across at the western sky
And I see the sun flaming red
I've a wish in me heart that me and the lads
Were at home and thinking of bed

At the end of a long hot day in the sun
As harvest-home we are bringing
Sat on the wagon all the way home
Legs ovver the side and singing

Looking out at this nightmare landscape
I think of the lads who are gone
Only me left now of our happy band
I've survived to sadly live on

Now evening's coming on and the western sky
Is painted with sun flaming red
I've a wish in me heart that me and the lads
Were at home and thinking of bed.

And soon for me now there'll be bullet or shell
No more of this bloody France

There'll be me and Dick, Harry and Tom
Jimmy and George and Will Chance

And we'll all be friends like we were before
Together like in the beginning
Sat on the wagon all the way home
Legs ovver the side and singing

100 years ago Jack Harrison won the Victoria Cross for single handedly taking out a machine gun which had his men pinned down at Oppy Wood. His body was never found. He is a legend at Hull rugby league football club where his record for tries scored in a season has stood for a century

Jack Harrison VC MC

This son of Hull from Southcoates Lane
A Boulevard hero many tries to his name
With Billy Batten he thrilled the fans
Chanting his name all over the ground

The western front and a morning in May
The East Yorkshire Pals pinned down where they lay
A machine gun emplacement, heavy fire from the gun
A lone figure stands and begins his run

Did he think he was at the Boulevard
When he jinked and ran fast and hard
This winger weaving and running his best
Across no man's land to a machine gun nest

That fatal day in Oppy Wood
When he gave his life for the common good
As in his brain the blood thundered loud
Did he hear the roar of the Boulevard crowd

Did he see the line at the Airlie Street end
And instead of enemies did he see friends
No pistol or grenade just a rugby ball packed
No German sniper just the Wigan full back
Did he aim for the line between the sticks
To ground the ball just right for the kick
But he silenced the gun that spat deadly fire
And it ended his life down in the French mire

And as the ref blew his whistle for time
Jack Harrison crossed that eternal line
A hero from the Boulevard he won his VC
So I learned in childhood at my grandfather's knee.

Inveraray

There is a monument to the soldiers
At Inveraray on the shores of Loch Fyne
It has stood there a hundred years
In sunshine, snow, and rain.

It is a statue of a soldier
In kilt and bonnet it stands
Commemorates two world wars
Those who died in foreign lands

As the piper skirls a lament
And the mist lays on the loch
The clouds dip down in sadness
Patrolled by osprey and hawk

And those lads who marched away
All those many years ago
Do their memories still linger
Upon this Scottish shore

Does a passing cloud recall
The fleeting sunshine smile
Of a long lost Jamie Douglas
Or a forgotten Willie McBride

And does the reflection in the water
Of fern fronds bending over
Mirror the tilt of the head
Of some brave young Scottish soldier

Or do the grasses in lowland meadows
Shifting restlessly to and fro
Quietly whisper the names
Of the lads who went off to war

And the sons that Scotland bore
Brought to manhood and then were lost
Will she remember them for ever
In her lovely glens and lochs

And as they peacefully rest
Beneath foreign marble stone
Do they dream in their eternal sleep
Of Scotland and of home

There is a monument to the soldiers
At Inveraray on the shores of Loch Fyne
It has stood there a hundred years
In sunshine, snow and rain.

Wilfred

A poor little lass in trouble
A baby on the way
No husband real or prospective
Not acceptable in those days

It was 1897
And to cover the family's shame
As soon as the child was born
He had to be given a name

Maybe the family assembled
And maybe they hatched a plan
And maybe they registered the baby
To her sister and her man.

The family loved that little boy
He was everyone's child they would say
Had a happy carefree childhood
In those far off Edwardian days

He lived at Thistleton Farm
Where Dove House stands today
Brought up with his other cousins
In the fields they would work and play

He grew up a fine young man
He was fearless and brave it is plain
Stood at Thistleton gate with a shotgun
Confronted a gang in the lane

He was only sixteen when it happened
Faced the dreaded Silver Hatchet gang
He chased off that mob of killers,
Who had already murdered one man

A year or two passed by
He signed on with the artillery corps
He was only seventeen when he joined
Marching off to war

They said there was never a bullet
Could kill a lad so brave
But that was disproved one day in France
And he went to an early grave

Looking back over all the years
I wonder what was it for
That lad who showed such promise
And was killed in the first world war

There are none left alive who knew him
One of a lost generation
But he's still mentioned in my family
With love and admiration

He's been talked of in the family
For a hundred years and more
The lad so beloved and brave
Lost in the war to end wars

Jimmy's Place

Its just a little homemade workshop
To help the heroes of yesterday
Old soldiers who once pledged their lives
To serve their country come what may.

To pass their time and try to forget
The things they have seen and done
They make little models of military things
Of soldiers and tanks and guns

They are the victims of conflict and war
And the nation is in their debt
Expected to be men when often just boys
And now they cannot forget

The state should be grateful but doesn't care
For those wounded in body or mind
So they help each other along the way
Forgotten and left behind

And they re-live again those days that are gone
Spent in Ireland, Afghanistan, Iraq
Telling tales of old mates and their exploits
And constantly looking back

That little workshop built by hand
They called it Jimmy's Place
Named for a lad who didn't come home
Killed at eighteen years of age

It's just a little homemade workshop
To help the heroes of yesterday
Old squaddies who once pledged their lives
To serve their country they say.

A Photograph Of Jack Harrison

A photograph is all we have left
Of Jack Harrison the gallant and brave
A photograph tinted in sepia
Enclosed in an old wooden frame.

He looks at us across the years
The trace of a smile on his lips
Proudly he wears his uniform
One gloved hand, the other hand, grips.

He sits there with quiet self-assurance
This classy winger for Hull FC
Nothing to prove, already famous,
Ready for the fighting overseas

No one can know his thoughts
As he sits awaiting posterity
Proud to serve his country
Prepared for war's barbarity

Did he know that he wouldn't return
To Hull and to wife and son
Only memories would remain
And gallant Jack would be gone

One act of outrageous gallantry
His life and safety scorning
And all that was brave Jack Harrison
Dissolved in the bright May morning

And now it's a hundred years on
Though the legend forever remains
All that is left is a memory
Imprisoned behind a glass frame

He looks at us across the years
A trace of a smile on his lips
Proudly wearing his uniform
One gloved hand, the other hand, grips

Parish Register

A dusty old book with sepia pages ...
Softly scented and soiled by the slow moving ages
Spine almost gone, covers bent and torn
The aroma of old paper, dusty and worn.

The title once was fine and the lettering gold
The book was treasured even though it was old
The history of a village held within its pages
People lived and died, recorded through the ages.

When the book was new, Elizabeth the First was on the throne
And village life continued as it had always done
A slowly paced progression from cradle to grave
And a man could live his life by what God gave

But pick up that volume and have another look
There is heartbreak and joy within that old book
A long awaited child, young lovers being married,
An untimely death, a loved one buried.

The times were so hard and children died young
And too often, it seems, the passing bell was rung
A single page records the death // of three little brothers
An unimaginable loss to their father and mother

And then inexorably the book moves on
Those same two parents had another little son
Then twins were christened and a baby daughter
Their lives blessed again with children's laughter

That dusty old book with its bare and dry details
Is full, if you look closely, of family tales
All people like us living in the same way
Who laughed and loved and cried just as we do today.

The healthy ones grew old if they had a bit of luck
And then they died and were written in the book
Just a name and a date, the entry short and sweet
A birth, a death, a marriage. A life now all complete

A dusty old book with sepia pages ...
Softly scented and soiled by the slow moving ages
Distilling our history, measure by daily measure
An old parish register, unassuming antique treasure.

Endrick Water

The bridge over Endrick water
Has stood there for three hundred years
On the road to Graham's castle
It is a place of ancient fears.

Walk from Burnside along to Craigend
A well-trodden path before
Imagine a Scottish castle
Eight hundred years ago

It was the home of Sir John de Graham
The laird of the castle so named
He fought with Braveheart in 1298
When Scottish independence was claimed

They were defeated at the Battle of Falkirk
By England's superior force
Graham was killed in the field
Blood spilled upon the gorse

They say that Braveheart himself
Carried his body from the battlefield
He kissed him and called him brother
And wept as there he kneeled

Graham is buried at Falkirk Church
Died for his country they say
Asleep in beautiful Scotland
With comrades who fell on that day

Continue on the east bank of Endrick
Follow the track to Ballochleam Farm
Pass to the west of the farmhouse
Shiver for fear of harm

But if the day is bright and sunny
And you're feeling brave in turn

Make your way to Inch of Leckie
Cross the ford to Gourlay's Burn

Look and see the ruined castle
Where Graham lived a life long gone
Look around you but do not linger
Find a reason to quickly move on

If the day is dark and brooding
If a mist lays on the lochs
Perhaps you feel uneasy
Among those lonely rocks

For maybe a memory of betrayal
Still lingers here in the trees
Recalling a savage and brutal death
And a spirit not at ease

The bridge over Endrick water
Has stood there for three hundred years
It leads to Graham's castle
A place of ancient fears

Sharon

A bonny young woman, both gallant and brave,
Just a hint of a tear in her eye
As she talked about her son
Who went away to die.

He joined the army when just a lad
Lived in barracks and polished his kit
Laughed with his mates, wrote home every week
And then his squad was hit

You could see she was proud of her son
Worth more to her than gold
And when he was killed in the desert
He was a lad just eighteen years old

It was an ideological conflict
Claimed the life of that young man
As he fought an unwinnable war
Far away in Afghanistan

And even one life is too many
To lose in a profligate war
Yet so many lives were lost there
And I wonder what was it for

And now that war is over
We decided to pull out after all
His mam is left with nothing
Just his photo on a wall

A bonny young woman, both gallant and brave
Just a hint of a tear in her eye
As she talked about her son
Who went away to die

Hot August Night

It was a hot night in summer
Just another night
No one thought it different from any other
Just another night

It was another night in summer
Simply another night
It was the very first day of August
It was just another night

On a summer's day six weeks before
An archduke came a-calling
But his life ended there on a city street
In Sarajevo the cards were falling

And a shot rang out on that summer's day
And the bullet flew fast and far
To Germany and Britain, to Belgium and France
In six weeks it travelled so far

And on a summer's night in August
A hot summer's night
On the first day of August in Europe
The protagonists lined up for a fight

And twenty million people died
From that bullet which travelled so far
And surely the sound of it echoes still
The sound of the First World War

It was a long hot night in summer
Simply another night
It was the first day of August 1914
It was just another night

Terry Ireland

Darkly Black
Volunteer
UNFOR
Esprit de Corps
Filling In The Paperwork
Veterans Breakfast Meet
Sword Of Honour
Playing The System
Organises Chaos
On The Shelf
That Status Quo
Legionnaire
Four Minute Warning
Guardians
For The Honour Of The Regiment
Escape
Drop-in Centre
Cockroaches
CCTV Extract
Soldier Of Fortune ii
Responsibility
Aftermath
Just Another Manic Morning
Blue On Blue
Soldier Soldier ii
Again And Again
Being Nonexistent

Darkly Black

We come in all different sizes
And in all different ages
And our varied ways of life
Are all at different stages.
Some of us are hale
Some of us are healthy
Many of us are poor
A few of us are wealthy

But what we have in common
We all swore that oath
Or, In old fashioned terms
We all pledged our troth
To stand for sovereign and country
No matter what that may cost.
Many of us of are mentally affected
A good few have limbs lost,

But abled or disabled
All of us have served
Not many get the respect
We feel they have deserved.
Some of us are young
Some of us are old
Some of us retiring
And some of us are bold.

We stand in our brotherhood
Help each other when we can
And all of us are proud
To call ourselves a Veteran.
All in different shapes and sizes
And no matter what we may lack
We all share our service and
A sense of humour darkly black.

Volunteer

Need volunteers in the Army?
Here's what they do
Just line up a squad and say
You, you, and you.
Nobody bothers to think
Or even to ask
Whether you have the knowledge
Or ability to carry out the task

Just assume you'll find a way
To carry out just what they say.
Write a report for the Depot O.C.
Just the task they handed to me.
Sat in the pub annoyed, drinking
I used toilet paper without thinking.
And, to make matters even worse
Wrote in couplets of iambic verse.

Signed Number Rank name
Date, and what's more
Drunkenly pushed it
Underneath his door.
Forty eight long hours of abject fear
As Monday relentlessly drew near.
The summons came and to my surprise
He greeted me with smiling eyes.

Said he was amused at my cheek,
Get it typed up for later this week,
Every squaddie has nine lives
But you just need to think on
With this latest little jape
Eight of yours have just gone.
Very soon after came the day
Training finished, I was on my way.

A much remembered experience
Of what the army could do
With the imperious finger and
The mouthed you and you and you.
Whether by luck or by judgement
I was never again anywhere near
When they were out on the prowl
Looking to appoint a volunteer
Eventually came the day
I was in a position to choose
Rank giving me the privilege
To impose those volunteer blues.
I tried to use it wisely but admit
I knew just what to do
To take a stroppy joskin and
Bring him down a peg or two.

UNFOR

Peacekeepers they called us
But we're just uniformed fools
Paying lip service to security
While terrorists broke all the rules.
That's my best mate
Sitting over there
Eyes fixed on the wall
In a long blank stare.
His body's all a tremble
He's nodding his head
I try to catch his attention but
His eyes are blank and dead.

That last street patrol
Was just one patrol too far
In his mind he's still seeing
That fast burning car.
The child he's holding tightly
As he smothers out the flames
The mother holding another
Screaming out their names.
Just innocent people
Who happened to walk past
Caught by chance in
That car bombs blast.

It seems to me he's in
A near catatonic state
So I guess for now I've lost
Another long standing mate.
It's down time now
A wad and a smoke
Somebody cracks
A spirit lifting joke
But my best mate is still
Well away from it all

That glassy eyed stare
Still fixed on the wall.

The medics are coming
They'll sedate him to bed
See what they can do
To sort out his head.
It just won't be the same
Now that he's gone
I'll miss him like hell
But this life still moves on
Back out in the streets we made sure
We didn't act without due thought,
Some trouser polishing johnny lawyer
Would've have had us up before the court.

Esprit De Corps

Vintage cyder was a killer,
It left the mind very clear
But somehow made the legs
Rather difficult to steer,
Which was why Old Scouse
Was contemplating the skies
Sitting gracefully in a ditch
With water up to his thighs.

I slid in beside him
Sat in the water too
For some reason it seemed
The right thing to do
And we talked of this and that
Until he said he felt Ok
Then we climbed back out
And continued on our way.

That's squaddie friendship
You just don't desert a mate
Though it raised a few questions
There at the Guardroom gate
As we stood there dripping
Having to explain
Our sodden condition
When we'd not had any rain.

Explanation accepted
Without the blink of an eye
And so off to the Billet
To get our civvies dry.
When you've lived in a billet
Learned how to share
Survived the odd beasting
Sweated blood on the square

Got to the stage when
You can't take it anymore
The squad will rally round
Pick you up off the floor
For the Army is the Army
And a friend is a friend
Through thick and thin
Until the very bitter end.

You'll maybe lie and deny
In the cause of his defence
Though in any other situation
It wouldn't make amy sense,
But you're loyal to a friend,
That's what friendships for.
It may be hard to understand
But it's called Esprit de Corps.

Filling In The Paperwork

You can't be an atheist in the Army
The recruiting sergeant had said
With that on a record any career
Starts off as good as dead.
No that's just not
What they like to see
Let's just put you down
As being C of E.
I didn't think it would matter
A big mistake I made
It came back to bite me
I fell out of Church Parade.

The Padre held a commission
Which I found rather sinister:
How could he be an officer
As well as being a Minister.
To me it didn't seem
To make any sense
But he treated my query
As being deliberate insolence.
So, I explained the situation
Which he certain wasn't buying
And we exchanged harsh words
When he accused me of lying

And not very long after
His anger was complete
When I stupidly suggested
He should be washing my feet.
They changed my records
And I again fell out at the door,
Never again being expected
To enter the church any more

I saluted the Padre's Commission
As they had a right to expect
But as for the man himself
I held not one iota of respect.

Veterans Breakfast Meet

There'll be black humour today,
Gentle ribbing, banter, and jokes,
Stripping away of egos, repartee
Among our mixed group of folks.
Bruising conversations maybe
But in a non-malicious way.
No place for the thin skinned
That's just not how we play.

It's the way it's done from
First moment of greeting
It's our irregularly held
Veteran's Breakfast meeting.
Some of us are damaged
But none of us are broken
Some carry hurt in their eyes
From experience unspoken.

Some have seen combat
Still carry mental scars
From frontline service in
The country's various wars
Some fought with a rifle
One fought with a pen
Each gave part of their life
As an active serviceman

The Padre's not a Veteran
But we've known him years
He's earned our respect as
He's listened to our fears
A range of ages gathered
For a morale boosting talk,
We've all worn the uniform
We've all walked the walk.

There are common experiences
That all of us have had
We're there for each other
In the good times and the bad.
It's a meeting of brothers
And we all know what to expect,
Ruthless character assassination
But with affection and respect.

We'll shake hands goodbye
Before each goes on his way
Feeling emotional benefit from
Our irregular breakfast day.
We're all looking forward to,
Though not knowing when,
We'll receive our invitation
To meet up and yarn again.

Just a couple of hours
of Banter forces style
Carrying each back
For Just a little while
To much younger times
From a very different past
When each passing day
Could have been your last

Sword Of Honour

His father was an Aristocrat
His mother a high class whore
And he attended Public School
As had his ancestors before,
Achieved a First at Oxbridge,
Sword of Honour at Sandhurst,
Served in Bosnian with UNFOR
Saw genocide at its very worst.

He resigned his commission
Following his service there
Couldn't cope with the memories
The sense of guilt and despair.
He dosses on the Streets now
A homeless hulk without a name
Disowned by his family and
Just seen as a bringer of shame.

The people on the streets
Try to avoid his eye,
Toss him the odd coin
As they pass him by.
He nods his head in gratitude
But he's not really there
As he copes with his demons
Behind his thousand yards stare.

All people see is a vagrant,
An alcoholic and a souse.
He's in Line for the title and
A seat in the Upper House.
Nobody gives a toss about
The many cases like him.
That's just the modern world
You either sink or swim

Come and join the forces
Show that you are willing
To go and serve your country
Accept the Old Queen's Shilling.
Learn to fight and kill
Sell your service on the cheap
And if you crack and break
You're out on the scrap heap.

Playing The System

Up before the R.S.M
Telling our agreed tale
The future of my mate at
Risk If we were to fail
You're lying Corporal
The Sergeant Major said
I didn't blink an eye, just
Kept staring straight ahead.
Entering phase two of
That recurring old game
Establishing the facts
And who's to blame.

Trying to establish whether
It was fact or just rumour,
Our Sergeant Major had
A broad sense of humour.
To save a mate
You didn't ask why
Just came out with
A most outrageous lie.
I thought i saw
The trace of a grin
A twinkled eye
A quivering chin.

No matter how unlikely
The story was you told
Sometimes audacity
Favoured the bold.
Any cat has nine lives and
You've just used up three
Remember that young man
Next time you're in front of me.
Fall out, be gone from my sight

You got the benefit of doubt
For an interesting story
But the jury's still out.

To protect a mate
You'd lie like hell
Sometimes you won
If you did it well
He'd seen it all
Been there before
Did he sit and chuckle
Behind his closed door.
The Father of the Regiment
Who set the rules of the game
And woe betide a miscreant
If he got to know their name.

Organised Chaos.

For just a little while when
Recruitment was very slow
And not long in the future
Conscription was due to go
A bunch of military misfits.
An almost unruly little mob.
Was chosen and recruited
For their very specific job.

Days of Mensa Tests,
Weeks of training courses,
Not really members of
The run of the mill forces,
Marshalled and ruled by
The Official Secrets Act,
Height of the Cold War,
Fear of the Warsaw Pact.

You'd see the Sergeant Major
Stand in obvious despair
As our little squad shambled
Over his sacred Drill Square.
It really must have been for him
A great culture shock
On the few occasions he visited
Our Operations Block.

Once through the Security Cage
Military protocol disappeared
To him it must have seemed
Almost civilian and weird.
Situated over a minefield,
Just needing to be armed,
An important little place
Where information was farmed.

Our ill-fitting group working
With NATO and the Yanks
Keeping very close eyes on
The Comrades and their tanks.
For just a little while they let us
Play our near anarchic game
But we knew eventually
Things couldn't stay the same.

They scattered the team
Split up the rule breakers
Imposed the greyness of
The rigid decision makers
For just a little period
They'd let us run at large
Until orthodoxy was reasserted,
And real soldiers took charge.

They took away the laughter
The joy at a good job done
The sense of delight at
A challenge faced and won
The work stayed the same
The sense of fun gone
And the military machine
Just ground inexorably on.

On The Shelf

They are out selling the poppies
In this run up to Remembrance Day
But they've confused Remembrance
With doing things the cheap way.

When I joined the colours, I knew
I could be sent off to war
I just didn't realise that
I wouldn't' be needed anymore
If I came back bent and broken
With scars deep in my mind
A future looking bleak
And my best years behind.

Oh, you paraded at Wootton Bassett,
Wept your tears for the dead,
And you wore your scarlet poppies
Coloured for past blood shed
But when my wounds mended
And I could use my artificial leg
I was thrown on the state
Almost like having to beg.

And such treatment is normal
For children partners and wives
Of all those who went to serve
And in duty gave their lives,
Or, worse still, survived
To feel the despair
Of being on the scrap heap
When very few people care

You call us all heroes
Just once a year,
Dig in your pockets when
Remembrance Day draws near,
And then seem to forget

That we are still alive
And for the rest of the time
We have to fight to survive.

They have to sell the poppies
For without Charity's help
This so called grateful nation
Has thrown veterans on the shelf.

That Status Quo

It was a contest of opposites
Charm and beauty versus brawn
Very consciously that day
Lines had been drawn.
The officer, dapper and slim
The ranker squat and square
Two different cultures meeting
As if fate had placed them there.
The only similarity apparent
That made the Officer sigh,
Each of them wore a monocle
Clenched tightly in one eye.

One of them small and slim
The best money could procure
The other NHS prescription
Basic, serviceable, and sure.
They stood staring at each other
One full of angst and outrage
One deferentially poker faced
Standing there centre stage
For long long seconds
They stood rooted in that place
Until with obvious effort
One did a quick about face

And sauntered nonchalantly
Off the Regimental square
Left a half inspected squad
Still standing to attention there.
The point having been made
The contest called a draw
Discretion being exercised
Monocle never worn anymore
The ranker relishing in
All the bets that he'd won

For daring to wear it
The way he'd just done.

Queen's regs being checked
There's was found no reason why
A ranker shouldn't wear one
To correct the vision in one eye.
To avoid future confrontation
Concessions were quickly made
And the ranker never ever
Wore his monocle on parade.
For an officer is an officer
And at all times must show
Necessary steps will be taken
To maintain that status quo.

Legionnaire

Just a quick notification that
A new resident was on his way
Gave us enough time to get
A room ready for him to stay
Not our usual type of client
A Veteran French Legionnaire
It was beyond my pay grade
To know how he'd ended there.

He was going through a crisis
In his domestic civilian life
Needed a break away from
His family and his wife.
The Veteran Brotherhood
Had taken care of it
Referred him on to us
For one of our bedsits.

He'd woken up in hospital
Physically sound and whole
The only surviving member
Of an ambushed recce patrol
With no recollection of how
He'd ended up there,
Or the three days lost that
He'd spent under care.

Discharged back to Blighty
Survivor guilt to the fore
PTSD setting in he just
Couldn't take anymore.
All this had happened
A good few years ago
But Traumatic Stress Disorder
Can take many years to show.
He stayed just a few months
And, not telling us why

He went back to his wife
Where he'd chosen to die.
Just days before he passed
I was surprised to hear his voice
When he rang me to tell me
Why he made that choice.

Said with Chronic lung disease
He was very near his end
And he wanted to thank me
For being both helper and friend.
Shocked and distraught not
Knowing what to say or do
I let Forces black humour
Help carry me through.

The Brotherhood is International
A mixed and disparate lot
So many times it's the sad case
Each other is all we've got.
Booted and suited by his box
We all took time to think
Drank a toast to his memory, left
Untouched the absent friend's drink.

Four minute warning

Four minute warning they said
At the height of the Cold War
Just exactly four minutes
Not a split second more.
Four minutes warning of
Nuclear missiles on track.
Enough time apparently
For us to fire back.
Having got the message
What would we to do next,
Grab our loving partners
And indulge in wild wild sex,
Then, if it was a false alarm
The panic of weeks or more
Hoping against hope our
Personal birth rate didn't soar?

Have that final little ciggie
Because prospects look bleak
Ignoring the hard earned fact
You'd just been stopped week?
Let the rising tension
Push you over the edge
And take a final Scotch
In spite of taking the pledge?
And then the powers decided
Four minutes was too long.
The common herd would
Just use the time all wrong.

They'd just puff and panic
Scream, cry, and shirk
Instead of just stoically
Carrying on with their work.
All the lost productivity
All the pain and terror
Just because that button

Was maybe pushed in error.
There's not even a minute now
They can't be bothered to try
The worthy will be in shelters
And the peasantry will just die.
It's called Survival Of The Fittest
It's nothing to do with being healthy,
It's just one of the many privileges
Of being ludicrously stinking wealthy.

Guardians

I heard the promise of freedom,
Became an eager volunteer,
Welcomed you to my country
When you arrived here.
Now, my world is in ashes.
My life in despair
I worked in your cause
But you just don't care.

You came here as liberators
Stayed here for twenty years
Then like all schoolyard bullies
Upped sticks and disappeared.
A chaotic withdrawal
But that's what you do,
Turn tail and run when
The going gets hard for you.

You broke all your commitments
As you left most of us behind
It seems to be a case of
Out of sight out of mind.
I am one of the very many
Victims of your thoughtless wars
Who believed in your intentions
And fought in your cause.

Disillusioned and in danger
I ask myself the question why
What did I do so wrong that
You left me here possibly to die.
All over so very quickly when
You decided it was time to go
And my world so very quickly
Returned to a past Status Quo

Because when all said and done
You seem to know no diplomacy
Other than that of bullet and gun.
And we join the millions of victims
Of yet another unfinished cause
As you return to Fortress America
From yet another unfinished war.

For The Honour Of The Regiment

It was a desperate situation,
Regimental honour at stake,
Decision urgently needed
As to what actions to take.
The Colonel was in paroxysms
The RSM was spitting blood
The M.O. was overworked and
Things just weren't looking good.

An outbreak of indiscipline was
Fast spreading through the ranks,
Squaddies dying without permission
Without a by your leave or thanks,
In such sloppy situations which
Caused the C.O. to angrily mention
They didn't even have the courtesy
To die properly lying at attention.

With ruthless Military action
With no thought of pity
Permission to die withdrawn
Without the relevant chitty.
Two weeks' notice of intent
Sent with an application
Was now the requirement
To sort out the situation.

Expiring without notice
Became a disciplinary offence
Combined with an appeal
To use their common sense.
Extra duties to be imposed for
Future unauthorised expiration,
The deceased's unit being held
To blame for the situation.

The system worked a treat
For any squaddie hates
Being held responsible
For letting down his mates.
The situation stabilised
Until finally at length
The regiment returned to
Fully operational strength.

Sanity quickly established
Thanks to the decisions made
And the Colonel and Sergeant Major
Held a celebratory Regimental Parade.
Pardons were quickly issued for those
Who'd died without permission
And the Regiment quickly returned
To its allocated operational mission.

Escape

Locked in the Valley of Darkness
Not seeing any chance of escape
Survivor guilt and bereavement
A constant form of mental rape.
Then the veterans stepped in
Dragged me on the Metal Bird
Back to a place of happiness
Years before we'd all shared.
A little bit of reticence
At our first greeting
More than forty years
Since our last meeting,

In that very village.
In that very space.
Old friendships just
Fell back into place.
And slowly and carefully
They brought me back to life
Helped me to finally accept
The sad loss of my wife.
When the Big Metal Birds
Sent us on our various ways
I was ready and more able
To face the coming days.

Out of the Valley of Darkness
My grief nearing its end
Thanks to the reunion
Of old Squaddie Friends
When you've shared the Beasting
Shared the pressure and the fears
Watched each other's backs
Friendship overcomes the years.

There were eight in the party,
Now we are down to five,
But one way and another we
Still help each other survive.

Drop-in Centre

There's Scottie in his chair
Tongue firmly in his cheek
Trying to wind up Old Noel,
The highlight of his week.
Noel, over eighty, Veteran
Of the Korean War
Gives as good as he gets
And dishes out much more.
Gordon's his visiting carer
Sits there with a big grin
Not himself a veteran but
He's managed to fit in.

Big Dave is eating as usual
Throwing in the odd word,
The vision of him ever fitting
In a tank now patently absurd.
Crann's the honorary caretaker
Helping out while he waits
For his entry Visa to join
His fiancée over in the states.
Emily the teenaged volunteer
Who won't take any lip
Has those hardened veterans
Under her slender fingertips.

Tuesday morning at The Centre,
Stacks of admin there to do,
Bur I've had to close the office
And get on with the brew.
It's not yet ten o'clock
The Drop-in looks nearly full
Already starting the craic
The banter and the bull.
So many other people coming
In and out in a steady flow

As one comes in another
Just seems to get up go.

Regimental rivalries
Black Forces Humour
Downright lies and
Manufactured rumour.
Hobbie's by the door
Taking the whole scene in,
Vic's chatting to Chris
Who's sat there with a grin.
That's the way it used to be
But now it's closed and gone
In a Covid changed world
Where things have moved on.

So many years we lasted
Existing from day to day
And then for some reason
We seemed to lose our way.
The rise of the Pandemic
Seemed to be the last straw
And the founding spirit just
Wasn't' there anymore.
The Drop-in that helped so many
Was just too good to last
Like so many valued things
Just a memory of the past.

Cockroaches

They were always present.
They ruled the kitchen by night.
You could hear them in the dark
See them when we turned on the light
Making kamikaze runs across the grill,
Hear them sizzle pop and roast
When you popped in for supper,
Make your own hot buttered toast.

They were hidden in the mash,
Even sometimes in the fries,
Floating in the soup urns,
Peeping out of hot meat pies.
Just a fact of billet life
You knew you'd never beat 'em
Just prayed and hoped that
You hadn't gone and eaten 'em.

Cockroaches in the cookhouse
A fact you had to admire
Constantly scurrying around
Never seeming to to tire.
A fact we learned to live with,
With comments a little rude
If you were unlucky enough
To find a dead one in your food.

You'd move it surreptitiously
Hoping not to spoil others scoff
A highlight of each day was
Each short communal trough.
We were young, fit, and hungry
And we didn't really feel
It was in the best of taste to ruin
Another's much needed meal.

I read they'd been on this planet
Millennia longer than modern man.
If a creature can survive extinctions
I'm sure that hardy species can.
In my honest option, for
Whatever that's worth,
They'll still be around after man
Has long been wiped off this Earth

CCTV Extract

A fire in the kitchen?
I smell of smoke in the hall.
Somebody is very guiltily
Washing down the wall.
What's left of the toaster's
Just a burnt plastic shell.
Sometime last night
We almost had a mini hell.

Thank the Lord for CCTV.
A bit of a disturbing sight
He'd come in a bit tipsy
Just after midnight.
Put the toaster on the hob
Switched the wrong device on
Seemed blithely unaware that
The smoke alarm had gone.

He'd sat drinking tea
Supremely unaware
Of the flames and smoke
Swirling around his chair.
A pajamaed figure appears
Smoke alarm must have alerted
Situation quickly sorted
Potential emergency averted.

White faced and anxious
Sitting with his dad and me
As we all sit and watch
The Closed Circuit Tv.
He'd been doing so well
Getting back on track
But, three steps forward
And two steps back.

Give credit where it's due,
Criticise where it's earned,
Put it down to experience,
Just another lesson learned.
Mending broken soldiers,
We all voluntarily chose
Win or lose it's a gamble,
Last night it was close.

Soldier Of Fortune ii

They put his name on a monument
One of the honoured dead,
I drank his health and started
The new life that stretched ahead.

We met by chance
In a very different place
This big genial Yank with
The generous smiling face.
One of those occasions
Nobody else could understand,
Two foreign bodies in
An unforgiving foreign land.
Initially working together
In a case of needs must
But ending in a relationship
Of reliance and trust.
Handshakes of respect
On the mission's ending day
As we each packed our kit
And went on our way.

He kept on reappearing
At various times of my life,
Once with his son
Once with his latest wife,
Joyous reunions with
A not quite friend
Fond goodbyes at
Each visit's end.
Hectic occasions
That we enjoyed so much
Always the parting promise.
To never ever lose touch.

That unbroken bond
Of experiences shared
The unspoken knowledge
That each in his way cared.

Then a strained phone call
In the middle of the night
His voice's tone telling me
Things weren't going right.
A long silence followed until,
Down the buddy grapevine
From a friend of a friend of
That not quite friend of mine,
One campaign too many
Disappeared without trace
My big Yankee pal with
The big smiley face.
A past soldier of fortune
Time now for me to move on
The last link with that life
Being now finally gone.

They put his name on a monument
One of the honoured dead,
I drank his health and started
The new life that stretched ahead.

Responsibility

I was a soldier in my time.
I was there by choice
I think that gives me the right
To exercise my voice.

We don't kill enough Politicians
When we get involved in War.
Perhaps we'd have more peace
If we killed a good few more.
Give every combat unit
Its own Member in residence
Send him on patrol
Let him actually experience
The death and destruction
His decisions can cause,
Make him risk his own life
In his Political Wars.
Let him live with the guilt
If he comes back alive
Make adjustments needed
For any Veteran to survive.
Perhaps war would diminish,
Diplomatic solutions willed
If more Politicians
Were sent off to be killed.

Yes I was a Regular soldier
A Politician's volunteer tool
Knowing I could be killed
By the words of a fool.

Aftermath

I did everything you asked
Obeyed every legal command
When as a teen you sent me
To that not quite alien land.
They spoke the same language
Looked just the same as me
But behind that appearance lay
A land of conflict and cruelty.

We stood out in the open
Uniformed on the street
Never sure of the reception
We were ever likely to meet.
Sometimes bricks and stones
Screaming their hate out loud
Sometimes bombs and petrol
From a rioting dangerous crowd.

They dressed in normal clothing
Hidden out there in plain sight
Sometimes we made mistakes,
Didn't always get it right.
Sometimes in stressful situations
We didn't always ask why,
Just acted in self preservation
Because nobody wants to die.

The terrorist, now freedom fighter
With much blood on his hands
Is now the politician in power
Holding sway over that land.
After so many long years
They want to step back in time
Bring me before a court
Accuse me of a war crime.

I did what was asked of me
Obeyed every legal command
As I struggled to survive in
That not quite alien land.
Now they're ready to sacrifice me
For a perceived political need,
But that's politicians for you mate,
A despised and despicable breed.

Just Another Manic Morning

Old Scottie's got a cob on
Can't find his favourite chair
Just back from a mini reunion
And he can't find it anywhere.
Not yet got the nerve to tell him
It went the middle of last week,
Mike gave it to a charity shop
When he had a fit of pique.

Martin's sat quietly crying,
Had his recurring nightmare
Of serving back in Bosnia
And he's in a fit of despair.
Almost time to open the Drop-In.
There's no cow juice in the fridge.
The centre without milk is like
A scene from Pork Chop Ridge.

Thirty seven coffees yesterday
And not a single one was black.
I've sent somebody to the shop
But they've not yet arrived back.
The centre for broken soldiers
And I'm the Duty Office nerd,
Just whinging and bitching
This morning is all I've heard.

They're all physically fit but
Their wounds are concealed
It's very unlikely some of them
Will ever be fully mentally healed.
Always the chance of a flashback,
An attack of doubt and fear,
And it can bring some relief
When a fellow veteran is near.

They've come back with the milk,
The mugs are lined up and clean,
Thanks be to the man who invented
The essential dish washing machine
It's almost Drop-In time,
The Duty Counsellor is on his way,
Noel and Gordon are at the door,
Time to start another manic day.

Old Scottie calmed down
Said he didn't really care
The Counsellor brought Martin
Out of his Bosnia nightmare.
The mugs all washed and clean
All ready for opening next day
The Drop-in's locked and closed
Time for home and I'm on my way.

Blue On Blue

They called it friendly fire
Then Blue on Blue instead,
But whatever they called it
The wrong people were dead.
There are pressures of war
Fears they need to hide
And trust to be maintained
In those on your own side.

It's a special situation in
Being a front line soldier
Without the added need
Of looking over the shoulder.
And there's the possibility,
With hindsight and past time,
Of a decision being made to
Accuse of historic war crime,
When the sharp suited man
With his acquired legal degree
Has the audacity to sit in
Judgement of people like me.

In pursuit of their so called justice,
While never ever having been there
And they dare, with no experience,
To judge conduct of those who were.
A decision made under pressure
Can later come back to haunt you
Decisions as bitterly regretted
As those that led to Blue on Blue

Soldier Soldier ii

They have an air of bravado
Confident but not loud,
Seldom seen on their own
Almost always in a crowd.
They seem to enjoy life
At a pace hard and fast
As though each day might
Just be their very last.

You strip a young person
Of the comforts of their life
Throw him into situations
Of anxiety and strife.
Never at times certain if
The next is his last breath
Train him to accept that
Occupational hazard death.

Outside of the forces
He's mostly an outcast,
Friendships from previous
Lives very seldom last.
He's probably seen more
Than most folk ever will
In all the various roles
He's been expected to fill.

The brotherhood of his service
That he's enjoyed all career long
With his engagement completed
Is suddenly over and gone.
Unless you've walked in his shoes
You just can't understand
The cost he's paid
In the service of his land,

And now he's a civilian
Facing a new life on his own
For the first time for years
Maybe he's truly on his own.
No more black billet humour
The comradeship all gone
Is it a surprise that sometimes
He stumbles as he tries to carry on.

So just cut him a little slack
As he tries to adjust
Try not to regard and treat him
With suspicion and mistrust.
He's given so many years in
The service of his nation
And the least he deserves is
Respect and consideration.

Again And Again

Do they still dig up bodies from
The killing Fields of Flanders,
Bones of those long ago
Enticed and betrayed,
Lost generation, sold and
Slaughtered for no real cause.

Do they inter those bodies
Amongst the precise rows
Of immaculate graves,
Each topped with it's
Serene white cross marked
With Number Rank Name,

Or the Unknown Soldiers tombs
For those as yet unidentified,
Those treated as cannon fodder,
The Butchers' Bill in life,
To be shamelessly and cynically
Too late honoured in death.

Did they learn any lessons,
Were promises made kept
Or are those Fields of Crosses
Just a sad and mute reminder
Of how easily it could and
Does happen again and again.

Once a year they parade their
National outpourings of grief
While, from the latest leaders
Crocodile tears shed as they take
Their annual break from Calculating
The continued profits of death.

Being Nonexistent

For forty years she stood there
On watch every single hour
One tentacle of defence against
A perceived enemy power.
There is now a new golf course
Where the aerial field once stood
They've long thinned and chopped
It's once concealing wood.

The Ops Block is the Club House,
The security cage and fences gone,
Presumably they removed the minefield
That she used to stand upon.
Very little recognisable now
Of the base that once had been
Only through the eyes of memory
Can the Drill Square be seen.

Disappearing under housing,
An estate of luxury homes
Occupying the spaces where
Guards and dogs once roamed
Cold War Warriors they called us
Behind our barbed wire fence
Our very existence denied but
An essential of our defence.

Told we wouldn't be coming home
If the Cold War turned hot
And nobody dared estimate
The survival time we'd got.
Of course it didn't happen
Barriers came tumbling down
Our Regiment decommissioned
Weeds cover the parade ground.

Forty years of non-existence erased,
Covered over by new household,
We are part of a Secret History
As the uneasy peace still holds.
Forty years she stood there
And I am very proud of course
That for a short while I did my bit
In that essential non-existent force.

Printed in Great Britain
by Amazon

32374182R00063